Can You Fill Our Shoes

Can You Fill Our Shoes

TOOLS FOR THE SHOES

Order this book online at www.trafford.com
or email orders@trafford.com

Most Trafford titles are also available at major online book retailers.

Print information available on the last page.

ISBN: 978-1-4120-7873-3 (sc)

Trafford rev. 06/18/2020

 www.trafford.com

North America & international
toll-free: 844-688-6899 (USA & Canada)
fax: 812 355 4082

Table of Contents

THE STRUGGLE
PART I

I was born Jan.28, 1973 to Emmitt and Earlene Davis on Bowdre farm in Robinsonville, Ms. There were five of us, four boys and one girl. I was the youngest of the five. My father was a farmer and my mother was a maid. Neither of them made good money; therefore life was difficult. My father left home in 1981 when I was 8 yrs. old, leaving my momma to take care of five children, my brother Emmitt, Jr., sister Patricia 14, (brothers) Thomas13, and Jessie 11. Emmitt was mostly in and out. He had a life and mind of his own. He loved his women, alcohol, and parties. My sister mostly kept the rest of us fed, and helped our mom take care of us. With her tomboy demeanor, she got her respect. She didn't believe in a belt, her fist was the first and last alternative. Tom was more of a quiet teenager. He wouldn't say much unless he was spoken to. Jay (Jessie) he was one who would do malicious acts to aggravate me. He and I did not see eye to eye for a long time. Fights would often break out between us. We would fight because I was the type of kid that wouldn't bother anyone and I didn't want anyone to bother me. I was more humble than anything. I guess I learned that by going to church with my mother every Sunday.

There were some Sundays that she only taught her children, but it never discouraged her. She faithfully brought her children whether it rained, sun-shined, or snowed. At one time, we did not have a car, and she would get on the phone and call members to pick us up for service. Regardless of what struggle we had, she never gave up on the Lord.

I don't know about my mother, but I began thinking, what use is it to serve a God that can do anything but doesn't seem to be doing anything. I often got frustrated with God because I only saw our family breaking apart. I didn't know it at the time, but God had it all under control.

Christmas 1981, was a sad one, because there were no Christmas gifts or dinner. The neighbors would come down and ask, "What did you all get for Christmas", while they flashed what they had gotten. We would think of something other than the truth.

In the summer of 1983, we were told by the farm owner, Pen Ewing, that we had to move off of his farm, because our father no longer worked for him. We were given (3), three days to move or be locked out.

That same month, my father and his girlfriend provided a trailer house for us. We moved in with no running water, no electricity, no gas, and no air conditioning. We worked many hours trying to clean that land and get that old trailer prepared for living. Cold water was later turned on, electricity was used from the house next door, and a very small propane tank was hooked for gas.

The summer of 1983 was such a challenge for me. Pest and rodents filled the trailer. Reptiles also made their way in through holes in the house. It was already hot in the house because there was no air conditioning, and those encounters just added to the frustrations.

Fall hit, and school began, and we dreaded it because

we didn't have sufficient clothing for school. We were embarrassed for our friends to come over because they were much more fortunate than we were; nevertheless, they came frequently and we kept going to school.

The winter of 1983 came and we were not prepared, because we had no hot water and therefore we had to boil water to take a warm bath. The heat that we depended on was only a very small space heater that sat in the corner of the house. Whether we were ready or not, winter came and we begin a long and cold winter. There were so many holes in the floors, walls, and ceiling that it was impossible to keep the house warm. It was just as cold inside as it was outside. Fog would come from our mouths when we spoke or took breaths. I laid down a lot of nights and couldn't go to sleep because it was so cold in the house. Can you imagine jut lying in your bed unable to sleep, shivering from the cold? I had never imagined having to go through that, but I did. Mornings were miserable, because we had to get up early for school in that ice box feeling house. All of us would gather around that very small space heater in the corner to absorb some heat. I would often get frustrated and walk away from the heater and bare the cold.

The Christmas of 1983 came, and if it's one time of year that I really love is Christmas, and all the joy that come along with it. But this particular Christmas was like any ordinary day. There were no toys, gifts, or dinner. The only entertainment was N.F.L. Football games. The children that lived next door to us were wealthy people, and they had it good. They had things I only fantasized about having. And the very thing I dreaded to happen, it happened. They came over and asked that very embarrassing, "What did you all get for Christmas", and I replied, 'Nothing'. That was such an embarrassment, but it came so often, until we got accustomed to it.

A new decade, 1990, came around and several more embarrassing times with it. By that time, I was a senior in high school and was preparing for an adult life. I made up in my mind that I wouldn't live like I had to before, and when I had children, they wouldn't have to live like I had to. June 6, 1991 came, and I graduated with honors from Rosa Fort High School in Tunica, Ms. Life was just beginning for me, but I took it head on.

There were not that many jobs at that time, only a pillow factory and a chemical plant. I went to them both and got the same answer; "We are not taking applications at this time".

In 1992, Drex-All Chemical called me and I began to work on the line for $3.35 an hour. The money was small and the supervisors were prejudice. I thought to my-self, I'm not going to be here long. One month later, the workers declared a strike for better wages, but I couldn't afford to strike, I needed work. I went to Pillowticks and was hired part-time. I worked hard everyday that I was there, but it didn't do me any good because of a lack of work. I was laid-off, and from there, I just did little pick-up jobs until 1993 when the second casino came to Tunica.

In August 1993, I began to work valet parking for the Lucky Lady Casino, a step up from what I had been doing. I worked until 1994 and then began working at Sam Town Casino on December 1994. I did multiple

4

jobs there up to 1999. Between 1994 and 1998 I took on other casino jobs to make ends meet, but I eventually got burned out with the casino work. The money was great but the customers were a piece of work and the system was just too much to ask for. We worked all weekends and holidays and were constantly watched, and their golden rule was, "The customers are always right." I did not think so, but there was no need to go anywhere else because if you've worked one casino, you've worked them all. The rules are all the same.

On March 15, 1999, I was hired as a jailer at the Tunica County Sheriff's Department in Tunica, MS. I continued to work as a line cook at Sam Town until August 1999 and continued full time at the Sheriff's Department. At $15,000 a year, I took a chance on losing everything I owned, but I knew the only way to become better and advance in the department, was to devote my time into that place alone.

Sure enough, I began learning the system and the do's and don'ts. On October 4, 1999, I was promoted to a Deputy in the Patrol division. I trained with several (F.T.O's) Field Training Officers and learned different ways to handle different situations. They tried their best to prepare me for my future.

On January 1, 2000, I was sent to the Police Academy. My reason for becoming an officer was to get good benefits and a decent pay so my family and I wouldn't have to live like I did when I was growing up. Moreover, I wanted to be in a comfortable environment and where I made a difference. We (officers) are stereotyped, but this why I became a cop.

PART II
A COP'S LIFE

M.L.E.O.T.A.

January1, 2000 I made it to Pearl, MS at the Mississippi Law Enforcement Officers Training Academy(BASIC CLASS #189), a place where only the top instructors teach and the top cadets complete. It was a place like I had never gone to before. I had heard the training was intense, the learning was plentiful, and the rules were quickly learned. Previous cadets had put me in the twilight zone about the facility. So, my heart was racing, thinking that every moment is subject to be the moment that enters us into it. We feared the smallest instructors as if they were cheetahs and you were gazelles. The moment arrived when we least expected it to, when all cadets are asked to come inside.

The director, who we did not know, walked up to the microphone. He was about 6'4" and 260 pounds. It was quiet as mice running on cotton because every cadet was afraid. "Good morning," he said with a deep voice. We were welcomed and the rules were given. Many of the rules were hard to accept, because there were so many limitations. Most of the rules only gave us one chance. They were tough, but they only meant discipline.

RULES AND REGULATIONS FOR BASIC TRAINING

I.   VEHICLES AND PARKING

Students shall park their vehicles in designated areas only. The designated area for student parking is on the Southwest corner of the skid pad unless otherwise instructed.
Students will drive personal vehicles only while traveling to and from the Academy, unless otherwise instructed. Seatbelts should be worn in all vehicles operated on the Academy grounds.

II.   TARDINESS
Each student is required to be punctual for all classes, meals, formations, physical training and other activities. Classes will begin and end promptly at scheduled times unless specific instructions are given to the contrary. Failure to appear in the class or scheduled function at the specified time will be considered a tardy. Tardiness may be charged at any time during the scheduled training day or for any required function outside the classroom.

The first unexcused tardy will result in additional duty, the second in an official reprimand and the third in a dismissal hearing before the Student Review Board.

III.   ABSENCES

A student may not leave the Academy at any time

except on direct order or special permission of the Coordinator, Training Officer, or Director of the Academy. A student may be allowed reasonable emergency leave when approved for legitimate reasons (sickness, court, and emergencies). The student must submit a written reason (as designated by the Coordinator) no later than the first day upon returning to the Academy. Any student, upon his/her return, must make up all classes and exams missed. During the last 4 weeks of training, a student may not have time to make up for lengthy absence. Students are hereby warned that they miss the opportunity to graduate with their class if they are unable to make up any classes missed. In such cases, the student will be allowed to make up the class work missed during the next basic training cycle and graduate with that later class. All students granted weekend leave or excused absence must sign out before leaving and must sign in upon returning. The Coordinator will specify the date and hour for return from weekend leave or other excused absence.

Failure to comply with any of the foregoing requirements will constitute an unexcused absence.

Any unexcused absence my result in a dismissal hearing before the Student Review Board. Likewise, any excessive excused absence my result in such a dismissal hearing.
If a student is absent more than 24 hours of classroom training during the 9 weeks of training, this will result in a dismissal hearing.

IV.   COURTESY AND DISCIPLINE

A. Chain of Command

Students are required to strictly adhere to the chain of command. The chain of command at the Mississippi Law Enforcement Officers' Training Academy starts with the Squad Leader and progresses through the Platoon Leader to the Coordinator to the Training Officer and up to the Director of the Academy.

B. Conduct and Discipline

Discipline is a way of life for the competent law enforcement officer. Students are to conduct themselves in an exemplary professional manner at all times. They must obey all lawful orders of the Academy Staff and others in the chain of command. Each student should conform his/her conduct to the rules and regulations in this manual. Insubordination or failure to obey any lawful order is grounds for dismissal.

Immoral or disorderly conduct will not be condoned. Profane, obscene, vulgar or indecent language commonly known as cursing or violent swearing will not be tolerated. Any student who physically or verbally assaults any other student or employee, except as required by a training class, is subject to immediate dismissal.

A staff member will point out minor infractions of the rules and regulations to the students so that the infraction may be immediately corrected. The staff member observing or having knowledge of the infraction(s) will report serious infraction or repeated minor infraction to the coordinator

C. **Dormitory Conduct**

Students in the dormitory shall conduct themselves in a professional manner. Rowdiness, horseplay, loud music, late hours, stealing, immoral or obscene conduct or any disruptive behavior unbecoming a student will result in disciplinary action or dismissal. All dormitory rooms and bays will be subject to inspection and/or search. A student should have no expectation of privacy in those areas. A student's request for admission to the Academy shall be construed as an implied consent to all necessary investigations, questionings, interrogations and searches. Academy officials or law enforcement officers engaged in an official investigation will conduct these investigations, inspection or searches. In additional to areas within the Academy buildings, all of the possessions of a student, including his or her vehicle are subject to search upon reasonable suspicion that said student is committing or has committed a violation of law or these rules and regulations.

D. **Dormitory Curfew**

A dormitory curfew for students is established at 2230 hours. All students must be in their rooms and quiet after that time. A bed check may be held at any time during the night. The upstairs lobby in the Administration Building is the designated recreation area for female students. Therefore, male students are not allowed on the second floor of the Administration after 7:00 p.m., unless they are in a class supervised or required by a staff member.

E. **Living Quarters**

Each student is assigned quarters which may be changed only when directed by a staff member. Each student will share in the proper policing of said quarters, buildings and grounds as directed. All beds will be made, shoes and clothing stored, in the manner prescribed. Foodstuff of any kind will no be kept or consumed in the dormitory, except in designated lobby areas.

F. Courtesy in the Cafeteria

Students are required to use proper table manners while eating in the cafeteria. Loud, boisterous or otherwise unruly talking will not be tolerated. As a student finishes eating, he/she will immediately police his/her area, place the tray in the window provided for same, and depart from the dining room.

G.Inspections

Inspections of bays, halls, stairways, latrines, living areas, classrooms, and person will be made daily. Each student will be expected to perform efficiently and satisfactorily in all their activities. On the spot correction will be administered by inspecting staff members; serious discrepancies will be handled by the Coordinator.

V.   UNIFORM OF THE DAY

All students will be required to wear the Academy uniform during the training program. The designated uniform shall be maintained in clean, well-pressed order at all times. Leather and brass will be shined. These requirements may be waived while students are participating in special activities (physical training, firearm training, etc.).

The designated headgear will be a baseball cap with M.L.E.O.T.A. emblem.

VI.   CLASSROOM OPERATION

Students shall maintain proper decorum while in the classroom and shall treat all instructors with respect at all times.

A student should raise his/her hand and wait to be recognized before asking questions in class. Any student who shows disrespect, make vulgar or disruptive remarks or engages in other activity deemed disruptive by the instructor shall be subject to disciplinary action.
Students are required to maintain classroom cleanliness. Each student shall be responsible for the removal of trash from his/her area, and for returning the tablet arm of his/her seat to the down position at the end of each class.

All students are required to take ample notes in all subjects. Notes should be plainly written in ink or typed and kept in the permanent notebook, which is issued to each student.

VII.   BREAKS

Each class, whenever possible, will be allowed a ten-minute break per hour of instruction. The instructor in charge will designate times for breaks.

13

Coffee and lounging facilities are located in the lobby on the second floor of the Administration Building. Food and drinks are not allowed in the classrooms. Snacks may be purchased from vending machines located in the upstairs lounge of the Administration Building and the downstairs lounge of the dormitory. However, these machines are off limits to new students until the Coordinator advises them otherwise.

Foodstuff of any kind may not be kept or consumed in sleeping quarters, classroom, gym, and library or downstairs lobby of the Administration Building.

VIII.   EQUIPMENT AND SUPPLIES

All students are held responsible for the care of equipment, regardless of whether it is issued to an individual or provided for general use.   Uniform equipment will be worn according to existing regulations. Identification tags will be worn at all times except when attired in gym clothes. Identification tags will be attached to the right shirt pocket. Until training is completed, these tags remain the property of the Academy and should be surrendered upon resignation. In addition, any time a student is on leave from the Academy, including weekend leave, the student should leave his/her identification tag on the pillow on his/her bunk while absent from the Academy.

> All supplies and equipment issued a student should be returned in good condition if the student leaves before the training program is completed.

IX. PERSONAL HYGIENE AND GROOMING

Personal hygiene and appearance shall not be neglected. The face will be shaved; the hair cut according to the Academy's policy, and clothing and equipment kept neat and clean. Each student is required to bathe at least one time each day or at any time the necessity arises.

X.   ILLNESS OR INJURY

In the event of injury or illness, the student is required to report same immediately to an Academy official so that proper medical care may be provided and a record kept thereof.

Sick call for routine illnesses will be 1:00 p.m. each day. Basic students and/or his/her department will be responsible for all medical expenses.

XI.   SMOKING – USE OF TOBACCO

The use of any tobacco products in the classroom is prohibited. Suitable containers for disposal of cigarettes must be used. Do not crush cigarettes on the floors or grounds or throw them into urinals or toilets. Smoking is prohibited any place other than designated areas and lobbies. Chewing tobacco or snuff is prohibited any place other than outside.

XII.   TELEPHONES

Use of the Academy telephones in the Administration Building will be restricted to emergencies only. When not in class or an assignment, a student may use the public telephone located in the downstairs area lounge of the dormitory or on the second floor of the

Administration Building to make and receive personal phone calls. Unless officially directed, students should not use the beige telephones (intercom), which are located throughout the facilities. Student should advise their family, friends and relatives of this rule.

XIII. WEAPONS AND EXPLOSIVES

Explosives (including firecrackers) are prohibited on the Academy property. Firearms shall not be kept in the dormitory. Upon arrival, all firearms are to be checked in with the Staff Counselor, who will secure the firearms in the Training Academy's Firearms Room. Any student who possesses explosives, who fails to check in his/her weapon or who is found carrying or displaying a weapon in the dormitory, the classroom, or in any area except the firing range will be subject to **Immediate Dismissal.**

XIV. GAMBLING – INTOXICANTS – NARCOTICS

Gambling in any form is absolutely forbidden on the Academy property. The use and/or possession of alcoholic beverages, including beer, are prohibited on Academy property. The possession and/or use of narcotics (excluding prescribed medication) are also absolutely forbidden on Academy property. The violation of any of the above will be cause for **Immediate Dismissal,** and, if a violation of law occurs, prosecution may result.

XV. VISITORS

While not in class or on special details a student may receive visitors. Visiting will be allowed only the downstairs lobby of the Administration Building between the hours of 1215 and 1250 and 1715 and 1750. Students should not encourage visitors and should advise their families, friends and relatives of this rule.

XVI. VIOLATIONS OF LAWS

No student shall violate any State or Federal laws, or any city or town ordinances while attending the Academy. Violations of the city or town parking regulations shall not be construed to be a violation of this rule, provided the offense is not repeated. Any student, who may be arrested for any offense while on leave or while at the Academy, shall report the matter to the Director of the Academy within 48 hours. The student may be subject to dismissal due to having been arrested. The student who fails to report an arrest to the Director will be dismissed.

XVII. CHEATING

A student who lies, cheats or steals during Basic Training will be subject to immediate dismissal. All testing will be monitored thoroughly. In lieu of outright dismissal, any student who is observed to be cheating during nay testing may be given a zero for that test, regardless of whether it is a weekly examination, a firearms record firing or a defensive tactics test. The student will be given written notice that he or she is accused of cheating and will receive a zero. The student may appeal this action through the chain-of-command to the Director, who determination is final. If the zero grade results in a student's failure from the Academy, the student will be eligible for a student review board hearing just as if the student had been dismissed for violation of the rules and regulations. This is the only situation in which academic failure from the Academy will entitle a student to a review board hearing.

XVIII. PENALTIES

Penalties for violations of any student rule or regulation will be based upon the specific penalty provided in the manual. In the absence of a specified penalty, the severity of the violation or the combined effect of several violations will determine the penalty. In addition, mitigating and aggravating circumstances as well as the student's overall performance will be considered.

General penalties may include, but are by no means limited to:

A. Oral Reprimand   B. Written Reprimand
C. Dismissal from the Academy

Extra duty may be assigned to the student in conjunction with either A or B above. The student's department head will be notified when either a written reprimand or dismissal is inflicted. In addition, a permanent record of the penalty assessed will go in the student's file.

XXIV. DISCIPLINARY HEARING PROCEDURES

When a student is charged with violation of a rule or regulation that may result in his/her dismissal from the Academy that student shall immediately be suspended from all training activities and must promptly leave the Academy. A dismissal hearing will be scheduled before the Student Review Board without unreasonable delay. The student will also be advised of the date, time and location of the Review Board meeting. The student Review Board shall be appointed by the Director of the Training Academy and shall consist of at least 5 individuals. Any student may waive his/her right to have a dismissal hearing.

Student Review Board hearings at the Mississippi Law Enforcement Officers' Training Academy are hearings to arrive at decisions regarding student behavior. These decisions affect the student and his relationship with the Academy. The procedures to be followed by all review boards are as follows:

A.Review board hearings are of a private nature involving the student and the appropriate review board. They are closed to the public.

B.The hearings are presided over by the chairman of the review board or his designee.

C.The format of the hearing will follow this sequence:
1.Presentation of the charge(s).
2.A call for the response of the accused to the charge(s).
3.Supporting testimony and information on charge(s) with witnesses for the Academy first.
4.Presentation of the testimony of the accused, witnesses and supporting information.
5.Examination and questioning by members of the review board follow both the presentation of the charges and the defense of the accused.

D.The accused may bring an advisor of this own choice to the hearing. This advisor may be an attorney, another student or a citizen at large. If the accused wishes to have legal counsel present at the hearing, he must so inform Academy authorities at least twenty-four hours prior to the hearing. The advisor may address the review board only at the pleasure of the chairman.

E.At conclusion of the hearing, the review board will consider all material presented. Its deliberation will be closed to all except members of the review board. The review board will advise the accused of its decision in writing as soon as possible.

A transcript or synopsis of the hearing will be made and filed in the Director's Office.

When a student is dismissed from the Academy for violation of a rule or regulation, that student may be readmitted, at the discretion of the Director, when to do so would not be dangerous or disruptive to training. Any student eligible for readmission will normally have to wait at least 6 month for acceptance to basic training.

TRAINING PERFORMANCE STANDARDS

Students are required to perform satisfactorily in **all** their training activities. Any student who fails to do satisfactory work will be dismissed from the Academy. Training performance will be measured in 3 areas; namely, academics, skill certification and physical training.

H.Academics
6.Each student will be evaluated on his/her academic performance by the administration of written examination. At least one exam will be given during

each week of training, usually on Friday afternoon.

7.The Board on Law Enforcement Officer Standards and Training (BLEOST) requires that every Basic student must graduate with a minimum academic average of 70% out of a possible 100%. Each student must, therefore, complete the entire course with an overall average of 70% in order to receive a **Successful Completion** certificate from the Academy. That same average is necessary to be certified by the Standards Board. Any student who fails academically, even during the final week of training, will not be allowed to participate in any graduation activities.

8.Pursuant to BLEOST policy, students who have an academic average below 70% after the second week of training will be place on academic probation. A student on probation will be given a reasonable time, not to exceed two weeks, to bring his/her average above 70%. The student who fails to do so will be subject to dismissal unless it appears certain that he/she will improve his/her academic standing before the class is over. Whenever a student has stayed throughout the entire training course and finishes with an average under 70% that student will be dismissed prior to graduation.

9.Students on academic probation and others who are in academic trouble will be required to engage in designated study periods. The Coordinator will arrange for study group assistance for these individuals with either Counselors, Instructors or other students.

I.SKILL CERTIFICATION COURSES

The basic law enforcement curriculum contains several skill courses in which each student must participate. A student must demonstrate proficiency in firearms training of seventy-five percent (75%), and eighty percent (80%) in defensive driving, first ad and cardiopulmonary (CPR) to successfully complete the basic course.

Successful completion of skill courses will be determined through the administration of written examinations and/or practical exercises. Specific requirements for certification will be given at the first class meeting in each course.

Other skill areas are presented such as radar, intoxilyzer, defensive tactics (mechanics of arrest), officer survival and side handle/straight baton (impact weapons).

Firearms training requirements are set according to BLEOST standards. Each student must achieve a 75% overall average on all recorded pistol certification courses. Students must also demonstrate safety in handling firearms at all times. Repeated unsafe acts with a firearm will result in expulsion from firearms training.

Any student who fails to qualify after forty (40) hours in firearms training will be allowed to repeat all day time firearms courses one (1) time in order to achieve a qualifying score of 75%. If this student does not meet the qualifying requirements he/she will be dismissed from the Academy.

First aid and CPR requirements are set according to BLEOST standards. Each student must achieve an eighty percent (80%) in each of these courses. Each student will be given a written test made up by the

American Red Cross in each of these courses. If a student fails any of these tests, the student will be allowed to take that test over one (1) time in order to achieve a required 80% to successfully complete the course. If this student still does not meet the requirements he/she will be dismissed from the Academy.

J.Physical Training

All students must participate in the physical training classes unless a student has a valid medical excuse from a licensed practicing physician. Students will be required to participate in the BLEOST physical training classes three (3) days each. Students will be required to participate in other physical training classes two (2) days each week.

1.Testing: The student will participate in two physical training evaluations as required by BLEOST. The physical training test will be administered during the 9th week of training. If any student does not pass the first test he/she will be retested during the final week of training. Any student who does not pass the final physical training retest will be dismissed from the Academy as required by BLEOST. A student must score 70% or better on the physical training test required by BLEOST.

2.Injury or Illness: Any student who has a valid medical excuse from a licensed practicing physician will not be required to participate in any physical training for the duration of the excuse. The excused student must still report for physical training at the designated time and place, and observe the training.

The student must be released by his/her physician before allowed to continue all phases of the physical training program. Any student who misses more than eight (8) days of physical training, regardless of the reason, is subject to dismissal. In addition, any student who is found to have falsified any medical information on his/her application, or has medical conditions he/she has not revealed to the examining physician, may be dismissed from the Academy.

In all cases where a student's medical condition may require dismissal, the student will be notified of that possibility. The student will be given a reasonable time, not to exceed eight (8) class days, to return to full training.

3.Defensive tactics: All students will be required to participate in all defensive tactics written certification test and must score 80% or better to pass. In addition to the written test, students must demonstrate the ability to perform all of the techniques in handcuffing, joint locks, pressure points, defensive counter strikes and neck restrains.

4.Gym uniform: The uniform for all classes conducted in the gym (unless otherwise specified by that class instructor) will be a white cotton, full length, round neck t-shirt. The student's name must be stenciled in block letters no smaller than 2 inches in height on the back of the shirt across the shoulder blades. Plain navy blue or gray loose fitting cotton gym shorts with no detailing or markings. During periods of colder weather students will be permitted to wear warm-up suits. However, the warm-ups will be either navy blue or gray loose fitting with round neck shirt with the student's name stenciled on the back across the shoulder blades. No detailing should be on the suit. The student will also be required to wear non-marking sole gym shoes and white cotton gym/athletic socks.

K. Defensive Driving

All students must participate in all defensive driving exercises and each student must demonstrate acceptable levels of skill in the following areas:

1. Backing exercise
2. Perception/reaction simulator
3. Lollipop simulator
4. Road course

If any student is unable to successfully complete any of the listed driving exercises within the allotted time, he/she will be allowed six (6) additional attempts to successfully completely that exercise and twelve (12) attempts to complete the backing exercise.

All students must pass a written certification test with a grade of 80% or better. If any student fails to pass the written test, he/she will be retested on time. If any student is unable to pass any of the four (4) certification exercises, or the written exam, he/she will be subject to dismissal from the Academy.

L. Failure to Meet Performance Standards

1. The student who fails academically will be dismissed from training as noted in A. above.

2. The student who fails to qualify in firearms training will be dismissed from training as noted in firearms training in section B. above.

3.The student who fails in first aid or CPR will be dismissed from training as noted in first aid and CPR requirements in section B. above.

4.The student who fails complete physical training standards will be dismissed from training as noted in C. above.

5.The student who fails in defensive driving will be dismissed from training as noted in section D. above.

6.The student who fails in defensive tactics will be dismissed from training as noted in section C-3 above.

7.   When a student is dismissed from the Academy for failure to meet performance standards, the disciplinary hearing process will not be used. Prior to dismissal, the student will be given an opportunity to explain to the Director why he should not be dismissed. If there has been some error in the administration, grading or recording of that student's examination, then correction of the error will be accomplished before further action is taken. If there is no error, the student will be dismissed and that dismissal is final. A dismissal for failure to meet to meet the performance standards will not prevent a student from re-enrolling at a future training course.

After the rules were given, we were escorted to the barracks. This is were we were taught to hang our clothing. You (readers) probably say, you already know how to hang clothing. Maybe that's true, but when you get there, the following ten weeks will be done their way. We learned how to make a white-collar bunk. From the head of the bed to the bottom of the pillow, must be 12". Where the sheet folds over the blanket, must be 6". From the head of the bed to the end of the folded sheet must be 18". The extra blanket must be folded correctly and an even 12". If the folds are one inch too long or short, it is wrong. We learned footwear alignment under our covered bunk. We were told that inconsistency or either of these lessons, will result in P.T. (Physical Training). Their favorite punishment, is push-ups. After being settled in the barracks, the ten weeks of fun and adventure (as they called it) began.

The night fell, January weather sat in, and signs of fear filled the barracks. It was quiet until platoon leader Roy Sockweel came down stairs and said " Flag Pole in five minutes." Everyone began gathering shoes and clothing running to get in formation. Every cadet got in formation around the flagpole in attention. "At ease," the instructor shouted. We were advised that somebody left a chair out from under the table. "Half right-face," he said. We began to do several types of push-ups (regular, wide arm, and diamond push-ups), so many that cadets trembled, and some fell down. We began jumping in place with both hands leaving our sides to above our heads and legs extending from beneath us to approximately 2 ½ feet out from under you, simultaneously.

"Get up", instructors said. They began to yell and scream in our face. Just when we thought it was over, he said the next exercise is the side straddle hop, encadance, which means unity exercise. We did 600 of those. After we finished, we got the message that we are not to leave anything out of order. We went back in and begin to take showers. Before everybody could get out of the shower, it sounded again. "Flag Pole in 5 minutes." Our pores were open and some were wet from head to toe. Another mental situation arose that we had to overcome. The process repeated. We were so fatigue, we just all fell into our bunks. We were cold and tired. I'm thinking, "is this worth it." Shortly afterward, "Flag Pole in 5 minutes." I thought, "this is what I call, a living nightmare." We all went back outside and got in formation. An instructor came out. It was quiet as we shivered from the cold. He advised us that he was just getting us together to let us know that he was our counselor. I thought, " It's warmer in the barracks, could you have told us in there?" But we said, " he's cool." We said that because he didn't (PT) us. We went back in, and finally, we got to sleep.

Before the week was over, several cadets left because they could not take it. I could see that far away look in their eyes. I knew they could not make it. They couldn't handle being away from home a week at a time, because they thought that she may not be alone. All cadets had heard about Jodi. He is a character in a blues song that will do **ANYTHING** to take your girlfriend, wife, etc. The X Marine & PT instructor often sing caters, but his favorite was "Oh That Jodi Boy." Some just could not cut the physical work, because day one happened everyday. The daily activities were the same all week. Everything that happened the first day, happened all week, plus, extra (PT) for whatever we did wrong. We were tested on Friday for everything we had learned or were taught all week.

Finally, the week was over. Friday evening, we were released to go home. A full two-hour drive back home seemed like forever. We normally made it home between 7pm-8pm. I was excited like kids in a toy store, but I was too tired to do anything with my wife and kids. They have sacrificed everything for my career. They have desires that needed to be met, but sometimes I was just too tired. There was not really much time left to enjoy. I had dirty clothes from all week, and my shoes needed shining again, and the time I had left went to the family. After the excitement died down, I was hit with what the kids have done all week because I was not there. The next day I rested. Sunday at 1 PM, the two hour trip was on the way again. Sunday evening we were back at the academy for PT, and the same thing went on for the next 9 weeks.

The thought of graduating from the academy was overwhelming. We had endured pain, suffering, mental abuse, physical abuse, stress and every other thing that came our way. We fought a good fight and we finished our course. Basic Class 189 was ready for the street.

Graduation day came and all of our families were there. We had a beautiful ceremony and everybody was excited that it was finally over. We were sworn in and became Mississippi Law Enforcement Officers. Even though we had gone for only 10 weeks, some Law Enforcement Officers go 16 weeks, 20 weeks, 22 weeks, and 28 weeks. They endure more than we do because we are in a small town and state, so the minimum standards are smaller than that of a big city. We are very well trained for the situations in this small town. The State of Mississippi has done its part, and we as law enforcement officers, were ready to do ours.

Complaining Citizens

We have been putting every effort into serving our community, the citizens, and tourist. We started by patrolling the streets mostly in high crime areas, but we manage to make our way to every residential area when we're able to. We respond to all calls in good time, and we're courteous in doing so. When a 911 call is given to us, we accelerate even more, just to assist our citizens. This serve and protect effort is sometimes destroyed by complaining and ungrateful citizens. A few of the citizens compliment us on our efforts, but for the most of them, nothing satisfies them. We are only accepted when we solve a crime or catch a criminal that has violated the complainer's family, and that's just for that moment. If we don't solve a crime, we are criticized, alleging that we are not trying to do anything about it. Let me clear this up, no agency will solve 100% of the crimes that occur in their city (county). It will be considered an exceptional job if 50% of the major crimes are solved. Not all criminals leave evidence, neither will there be a witness around all the time. Sometimes criminals wait until they catch a victim in a secluded or wooded area. We're not all seeing and all knowing, we can't see everything, hear everything or get information on everything.

If we solve the crime, than people should be thankful, and if we don't, they may as well, chop it up as a lost because we will not solve every crime whether people think we should or not. There are rules and guidelines that we must follow in doing police work. Someone may have information about a crime and we may know that they do, but we can't scare or beat information out of them. It is unethical and unconstitutional. As much as we would like to solve every crime, if there is not enough evidence, it will not be a conviction in Court. In fact, the District Attorney will not take the case. Complaining all of the time will not change the outcome.

Some citizens complain about us not patrolling their areas. Citizens that live in quiet areas out in the country parts will not see us as much as the high crime areas. We are short in staff, so, we must secure the areas where there are plenty of drugs, burglaries, fights, stabbing, and shooting, and then we'll take the not so urgent call. We will help someone find a pet, but it must be after we have been very visible in higher crime areas. We are often short of staff and we have to spread our presence the best we can. Not only will we jeopardize the lives and property of citizens in high crime areas, but also it endangers the lives of officers on the shift with us. If two units patrol the rural areas and leave only one or two in the high crime area, then we are asking for trouble. If something major happens, an officer is more likely to go down or get killed. I won't have that on my conscious, that I left an officer and he gets crippled for life or gets killed because some of our citizens want it their way, right away.

There are children that expect their dads to come home and wrestle, play sports or whatever their hobbies are. Wives have needs and desires from their husbands that no one else can fulfill. I couldn't face an officer's family if he's killed and say, " I left him because of a citizens personal interests." We are often criticized for our work. If we're not the officers that people expect, there is no need to request our services. If they want us to be so much more visible, then they should encourage their relatives to become better citizens and apply or move into a high crime area. Until we are heavily staffed, we cannot be seen as much as the high crime areas. If some citizens would like to see more officers on the streets, moreover, see our duties done better, than there are job openings at the department. We are complained on for harassment. We are not out there to harass anyone. Everyone that lives in the (HCA), can get use to us being in that area. Most of the complaints are coming from the criminals. If they complain to our superiors enough about harassment and making threats to sue, sometimes we are moved from the area to keep down confusion. When this occurs, that gives them the opportunity to make their drug transactions, burglarize a home, or eliminate their competition. Their selfish desires cause them to make complaints. Sometimes we are there for a welfare check, but our presence intimidates them and it cuts their business. If a person don't live in that area and they are constantly riding through making circles and nowhere particular to go, they will be stopped and checked out. The law abiding citizens can not feel safe if we are never around, but the law breakers are not concerned about them because they are only interested in their own lust and filthy desires.

Some people complain, saying, "we're always stopping people." For starts, that's part of our job description and if our sheriff or chief says write tickets, violators will be stopped. If we do not stop cars, we will never catch hardcore criminals. If we do not catch them, do you know what? They will strike again and the next time they feel they need to rape or kill someone, it just may be you. If they commit a felony offense and flee to the next state, they will probably drive.

If they commit a road violation, then they will be stopped and ran through the computer. Whatever they have done, the computer will tell it. If we find that they are wanted, they will be apprehended, and that 's one more sex offender, robber or killer that will be taken off the streets. Just because people get stopped, that doesn't mean they will be treated like a criminal, but on the other hand, just because someone is not a criminal, that does not exclude that person from a citation. People should not complain when they know they were wrong? Some people are so self-righteous that whatever they do is right to them. We do not want to harass anyone. We wish that we could just ride and listen to the radio all day and night and then go home, The more we come into contact with people, the more our lives and health is a risk. We will never recover a vehicle if we do not stop suspicious looking cars and people. Complaints are so plentiful in Tunica County. In the year 2000, I had to go to internal affairs three time in 6 months and the parents initiated two of those. There are parents that make allegations that we are harassing their son(s). Most parents either do not know what their kids are doing or do not care, because they mostly take their child's word for it. That, " I don't be doing nothing, they just be messing with me." I know the penalty for harassing someone. I'm not going to get discharged or sued just to see a law breaker in jail. I do not have an interest to harass anyone.

According to my experiences, parents have believed whatever their child has told them. Those type of parents will forever have heartaches and pain. They can smell the marijuana scent on him, they can see the fear in his eyes and the handgun he carries, but they are in denial. When they have the smell on them, they are marijuana smokers and or sellers. We know the sellers and smokers because we have found it on them before. They know that we are on to their lives, and that is why they are afraid and they run. They are troublemakers in the streets and pretend to be angels at home, and parents have trouble believing what they have heard about their child. Nothing goes on in the streets that somebody has not heard about. When a criminal upsets another person, whether the other person is a criminal or not, all of a sudden, the department has another confidential informant (CI). Another thing, we will not apprehend anyone without cause. If a person is picked up on warrants, then that is a judge's order. That person has done something unlawful if a warrant has been issues for that person. Some kids are addicted to marijuana, which is causing their behavior to change. They are becoming violent and are stealing to support their habit. They are betraying to be a sheep, but they are wolves in sheep clothing. As soon as some parent's child gets into trouble, they immediately bail them out of trouble. They often loose creditability with officers to defend their child when there is plenty of evidence right before them. If they keep putting their neck on the line for their troubled child, it will be their heads that get chopped off. Parents will go to the extent of hiding their child in the house when they know that he has done wrong, and if they are not careful, they will be charged with aiding a criminal. Some parents are asking for trouble by covering their kids when they are wrong. If a child killed someone and the kid tells the parent, and the parent does not say anything, she is guilty of aiding and abiding.

Just because we are in a uniform, with a gun and badge, this does not mean we do not have feelings. I can't help but to think, if a cook puts everything he has into cooking his foods and making sure it is hot and just right, and then a customer says that the food was nasty and cold. How would he feel? Housekeepers, how would they feel if they stretch those sheets so that no wrinkle would be in the bed, and they are always accused of making wrinkled beds and leaving trash in the rooms? Ask yourself, how would they feel if someone complained on them all of the time. Dope dealers have feelings too. They may try to hide them, but they have them. How would they feel if every time they pick up their dope, they get large quantity, they sell it fast, they have special customers, they return twice as much money and less product than any other buyer, but every time they look around the King Pen says, "They are not doing enough. He may say the new kid on the block is turning more product than his right hand men.." Ask one, how would they feel, when they are ducking from the cops left and right to make sells and that's all the King can say is they are not producing. No one I know would trade in their $200,000 a year business or career for a $20-$30,000 a year badge and gun. We accept the low paying cop jobs, so there is no need for people to criticize us when we are protecting them while they make double or triple our salaries. Doctors and lawyers work are not as dangerous as ours. Both of them get the after mass of what we deal with. We appreciate their work, and hopefully they appreciate ours

Life and Death Situations

There are times when we are put in situations where we are going to live or die, and I plan to go home everyday to my family. There are some people that go down easy, but some go down fighting and shooting. They will not stop until there is a fatal blow. Sometimes a simple traffic stop turns deadly. When we stop a vehicle, we don't know who they are or what they're capable of doing. In the summer of 2001, one of our officers was dispatched to an accident at old highway 61- moon landing highway and when he got there, there he was expecting to work an accident but when he arrived, one of the drivers of the accident begin shooting. He had been sitting and associating with the officer. Our officer came out, but the suspect died. This was the same guy who had been coming to his house and talking to him. We often deal with people that will greet us one day and kill us the next. The same people that we went to school with and partied with will change from good to bad, and if we don't be careful with them, we could end up wounded for life or dead. Many officers are dead because they drop their guards. Officers have to be careful at all times. If a suspect put his or her hands in their pockets, an officer must make them get their hands out. That is a deadly act. If a suspect hands are visible, and in a safe place then they cannot hurt an officer. The hands are what does the killing. Sometimes our job require us to be put in a deadly situation, but there is no need to endanger our lives by letting a suspect put their hand where we can not see them.

There are times when officers are on a traffic stop and there is a good respectful driver. In Etton County, Wyoming on February 24, 1996, a driver is asked to come out of the vehicle for an interview. He then began to yell watch out! A driver came through on the icy ground and hit the police cruiser that nearly hits the stopped vehicle. The fact that the officer's sixth sense told him to put themselves out of harms way, they lived to tell someone about it.

Sometimes it gets really dangerous. In Los Angels, California, officers responded to a bank robbery in progress. When officers arrived, the very unexpected happened. A shootout occurred and suspects and officers were injured and some killed. The officers were put in a situation that some of them did not come out of. Many bullets were fired and several people were hurt and some were killed.

We are placed in dangerous positions at time, the kind that make your heart pound and race. We are sometimes put where only the safe and cautious officers survive. Some positions cause us to be so afraid that we have second thoughts about responding to the call, but it is our duty and we know someone is depending on us for help. Do not let anyone tell you that cops are not afraid at times, but we cannot allow our fears to overcome our duties.

Sometimes officers are put in positions where they do not know what to do. When shots ring out from a crowd, we do not know if someone is being shot or if we are being shot at.When they hear bullets bouncing off of the payment, that's enough to make an officer's heart race and their adrenaline pump. Their head will begin to fill up with questions/ who is it? Where is it coming from? When do we return fire? If so, where to? Has someone been shot and when it is discovered who is responsible? We cannot just fire into a crowd. If the shooter begins to get away, we cannot just let him get away, because others will begin to commit crimes openly. We are at times put where we cannot do anything even though we want to.

When a kid decides that he's going to rob a convenient store, and we arrive while the robbery is still in progress. We have to make the decision of getting shot by a kid or shoot the kid. I don't know why a teenager would do something so bad, but I do know if I find myself stairing a teen in the face and he has a gun that he is refusing to drop. We can't let him/her get away with the crime, and if he/she attempts to raise that weapon, they will be shot to stop the threat. These types of crimes changes from juvenile crimes to adult crimes. They're no longer teenagers when they make the crucial decision of robbing something or someone.

When we make the scene of an accident and a person is injured very badly. Their body is twisted and pinned. They are crying and begging us to help them. We can hear blood gurgling in their throats. We know it will cause more damage if we move them. We will ask ourselves several times, should I move them? Should I help them? Then we have to come to the realization that we're not fully trained in medical services and we just have to wait until help arrive.

Most accidents that happen in Tunica MS have resulted in severe injuries. We have made scenes and they were horrible. People were twisted and pinned, crying and begging us to help them, but we knew if we had moved them, we could easily do more damage. As an officer, naturally we desire to help people in that type of situation, but those desires quickly leave when we think of the risk of hurting them more.

Not all the time is the officer in life or death situations, but we are there when someone else is. The mere fact that we cannot help them bothers us. We know we are trained to go in and out of deadly situations, but others are just victims of circumstance. Sometimes they are at the wrong place at the wrong time.

When a carjacker decides that he is going to take a car, he does not look to see if there is a child in it. He just takes it. You can imagine the fear on that parents face as he blows intersections and swipe cars. Sometimes those drivers want stop until they fatally hit something.

When an officer engages in a pursuit, there are several questions that goes through our minds, along with those questions comes consequences: Do I get close enough to shoot the tire(s), and risk the chance of a bullet killing that child? Do I get close enough to bump it, causing it to loose control into oncoming traffic? Do I wait until it stops, and will that be too late? With all the questions to choose from, the right one has to be made.

When a felony occurs that result in a vehicular pursuit, the public focus is primarily on the officer's action. While an officer is trying to do the victim and the community justice by trying to apprehend the perpetrator, and inadvertently has an accident, then the finger is pointed at the officer for being negligent. The public then forgets temporarily about the crime that was committed. It seems as though the officer's life is not important. We cannot help but feel that we are the victims in society.

With the many situations that cops are placed in every few seconds, the right decision has to be made, because if we make the wrong one, it can cost us our jobs, sanity, career, a lot of money, prison time, but most of all we could lose our lives. Every decision is crucial whether it's under a calm situation or a intense one, so we do not need added pressure. Some situations

39

that have occurred with an officer have cost them their lives. They made a decision under pressure. It was the wrong one and it caused them their career, a big lawsuit, and some prison time. They could not handle the thought, so they end it all with a 40-caliber bullet to the head. Not all the time is the acts intentional. The officer even admits sometimes they made a mistake, but mistakes are costly.

The life and death situations are very risky. We put everything we have on the line for some people who will cross us out for a piece of a settlement. When we are chasing a robber who has just killed a person, and in the process of ending the chase as safely as we know how, we can get involved in an accident that hurt or kill someone else, and for the moment the robber-murderer has gone out of the window. The finger is now being pointed at the officer but he was just trying to do the community a favor by apprehending the killer. But most people forget about the guy that robbed and killed the old lady, their concern now is to sue the officer and his department for wrongful death. Who are the victims in society, officers are. No one cared about how officer's lives were endangered during the chase, how they avoided other accidents.

PART III
ON THE STREETS

A Sight for Sore Eyes

I had finally begun my career as a law
enforcement officer. The summer of 2000, we began
our shift and we were ready for whatever came our
way. Well that's what I thought until the dispatcher said
routine to White Oak road for a 10-50 (accident). When
I got there, a man had been thrown from his SUV into a
ditch and his leg was broken. The leg was broken from
the hip and twisted around. The elderly man, Paul
Pilgram was crying and praying, "Lord please help me,"
"I'm hurting." The expression on his face was very
painful. The driver who was also injured was crying
because he desperately wanted to help him but he was
hurt to. Bill Atkins cried like he had intentionally hurt
his friend but it was just an accident. I had never seen
anything disfigured before on someone's body until that
day.

Early one evening in 2001, we were patrolling
Highway 61 when a call came over the radio to routine
to Kirby Rd for a 1050 rollover, with injuries. When we
got there, a four-year old kid, Marvin Taylor, was a
victim of a DUI driver. The DUI driver was the person
he was riding with, that did not have him in a seat belt
when the accident happened. The boy's brothers were
just scratched and bruised up. Marvin looked O.K.
Until I looked at his wrist, I noticed a severed wrist,
with blood and torn tissue. At the center there were two
broken bones that were shaped liked the letter "Y."
Only the white tissue from the wrist held the hand
together. The little boy's hand dangled as the doctors
tried to place it on a supporter. Tears streamed down his
face as he endured the pain.

When I went home, I grabbed my children and
hugged them. I was saddened that this had happen to
that child, but I am more than grateful that it did not

happen to my two sons and daughter. We see children often that are hurt or killed by the hands of adults, but sometimes children do it to themselves.

In the fall of 2001, an 18- month old child was curious of what was cooking on the stove, so he opened the oven door. While the noodles were boiling, the kid climbed on the lightweight stove with his other brother and tilted the stove over. The hot water hit both kids. One of them, Michael Gordon, received 1st degree burns and the 18-month old child, Terry Gordon, who was dark complexion, was turned pink all over, and blisters covered the child. The mother was not watching the children when the incident occurred. It disturbed me because I thought, "What if that was my son?" I would not understand. Everything that goes on with children it makes an officer upset, because a lot of the times, the parents are negligent. Anything that goes on with the children, it hits home. Sometimes I find myself calling home to make sure everything is O.K.

There are adults that suffer serious injuries also. People are hurting and when we are trying to help them, regardless of how much we attempt to help, we are criticized. We risk our lives for some ungrateful people. We have seen things that make people value life more, things that we sometimes go home and dream about. We are sometimes put back at the scene where a person was dying. We are trained not to take our work home, but sometimes it follows us home. We sometimes make decisions that cause us to feel bad and the same feeling occurs in my dream and it doubles when I returned back at the scene.

Everyday we risk our lives and deal with the nightmares for people who do not appreciate it. Just because we wear a badge and guns, that doesn't mean that, we do not have feelings. We like to hear that we are doing a good job sometimes.

In 1997 Tunica Deputies were dispatched to Old Highway 61 for an accident involving a small passenger car and an18 wheeler. Deputy Barns and Don responded. Barnes said he knew it was fatal, so he accelerated over 100 miles per hour. At that speed, a stray dog can cause a vehicle to loose control and cause serious injuries or death. When he arrived, it was just as he thought. An 18-wheeler with a flat bed on it was parked partially across the road when a small Buick Century plowed right under it. When he walked up to the car, he said he saw a lady's body from chest and down. The flat bed of the trailer decapitated the lady. After the wreckage was pulled apart, the victim's head was found in the rear of the car. The coroner then recovered it and secured it into a body bag.

One early evening, the day was quiet. The dispatcher said 10-50 White Oak road and Prichard road with injuries. Shortly afterwards, she said the vehicle is engulfed in flames. Sirens were screaming and lights were flashing. Upon arrival, we could see the burning car and at the same time a few screams cried out for help but the vehicle was in too bad of a shape. Shortly after the few screams, everything got quiet. They had perished in the fire. One died from impact, and the other in the fire. The smell of burning flesh was in the air; therefore by-standers began to loose their composure. By the time the fire department got there, the bodies were burned beyond recognition. Not all the times will tragedies be strangers.

    Shortly after swing shift began, the dispatcher
said, "10-50 on Fitzgerald Blvd. and Casino way with
multiple injuries." I was working in another area so I
did not make the scene. I heard a request for the
accident investigator. That meant someone's dead. The
fatality set in my mind. And I wondered who it was.
S0-28, my call number) routine to the funeral home and
stand by the investigator told me, so I stood by. He said
prepare to identify the parties from the fatality. I
replied, "10-4 (copy)." The coroner and the funeral
home director arrived and asked me to help get the
three dead bodies inside the funeral home. After getting

them inside, the bags were unzipped. Two of the three were from my hometown.

The young lady was one whom I went to school with. She was 26 years old and had very young children and one was a girl. The young man was just 21 years old. His body was badly broken. Almost every bone in his body was broken. His body was like a rag doll. When it was picked up, it bends everywhere. Sharla Bond was from a large family. The family got the news and they all came to the funeral home crying and screaming. I had to stay to try and comfort the family. It began to disturb me because I knew the family well. I identified the bodies and then a family member stopped me. She asked as she wept, " Officer Davis, is it really her?" Slowly, I answered, "yes." Then the whole family began to scream and cry all over again. I eventually left because it was too much for me to handle.

This is the type of situation that officers have to deal with on a daily bases. It was late graduation night in the summer of 2000. Our Sheriff ordered a road block expecting to get D.U.I's. Well, while waiting on drunks, my god son who had just graduated 4 hours prior came through the road block. He was driving and three of his friends were with him. I spoke with him briefly. The last thing that I said to them was, "put your seat-belt's on." In the early morning, shortly after midnight, my godson Darrell was trying to get back to pick his uncle up from work. He was tired because he had been running all day preparing for his graduation. He fell asleep on Highway 61, crossing the centerline and went head on with another vehicle.

He was the only one that died. His face was disfigured
and body parts were broken. He was a respectful young
man who had given his life to God. He had a newborn
son who he tried all to take care of. He was a platoon
leader in the Jr. ROTC. His goal was to become an
officer. He previously said, "If I do not make the armed
services, I want to be a cop like you." It seemed like the
bad children live, and the good dies. Ask yourself,
could you handle our job.

　　I have heard a lot of things. I have smelled a lot
of things, and I have seen a lot of things. But nothing
compares to what officers have to hear, smell, and see
while they are on shift. We have been to some of the

weirdest situations. It is amazing how men, women, and their children do each other. I have seen men that tell their wives that they are not to use the phone and no access to society while they are gone. Not only do the women get treated badly but there are women that mistreat their spouse. They tip around on the men with other guys and girls. The men are sometimes suspicious of something and when they find out, it really breaks their heart. Have you every seen a grown man break down and (cry)? I am not talking about a small one; I am talking about a big 6'2" tall and 250lbs man. It's heart breaking to see a good man who tries hard, and gets the short end of the stick from his wife. You can't help but feel his pain.

Not only do parents say and do things to each other, but sometimes it is the child that causes the problem. They tell their parents to shut up and curse them as if they were adults. They tell their parents what they are not going to do. Until I got enough, I watched children bring tears to their parents' eyes. I thought to myself, that couldn't have been a child of mine. This comes from a lack of discipline and letting them have their way all of the time. We have made scenes where children have pulled knives and guns on their parents and left before we got there. Sometimes it's to late when we arrive. Their biological parents were killed at their hands. Could you even imagine that? We can't help but think, will our son(s) take the same idea and try to murder us?

There are teenage parents who have babies and they do not take good care of them. We enjoy kids. May 2001 we made a scene and the baby was crying because of the disturbance and the fact that it needed to be cleaned. I picked up the child and tried to comfort him. When the child was picked up, the smell that came from it was breath taken. And it is not the child's fault; it is the parents' fault. It smelled as thought the child's pamper had not been changed in days. Milk and vomit had settled in the child's clothing and under his neck. I could see at the bottom of the pamper lining that the child had defecated on himself and had dried up around the edges. His little head smelled like vomit. This is heart breaking but what you are about to read is breath taken.

We have been called to disturbances often, but no two disturbances are the same. Sometimes there is just arguing, scratches, but at other times, it is serious. What we see make us grit our teeth to help maintain our composure. On March 20, 2002, a girl and a woman had gotten into a fight over a boy. The woman was getting the best of the girl until she pulled out a straight razor. She cut the woman repeatedly. The wounds were long and deep, so deep on the arm that the biceps were laid open from each side, all the way down to the bone. The forearm was the same, about an 8-inch cut that we could see blood, tissue and bones. Above the waist about 2 inches, little Keisha cut her a new waist line. Blood covered the white t-shirt and blue pants, and her shoes were even bloody. It looked like something from a horror film.

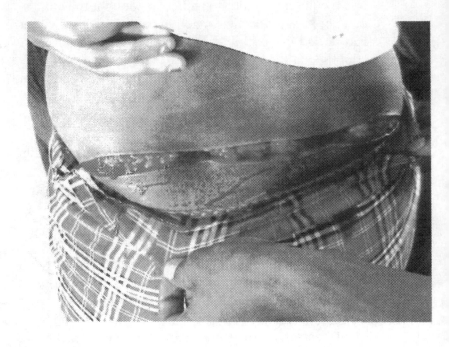

When this type of activity happens, it is us (officers) who have to take the chance of getting cut just to apprehend the suspect(s). When someone's enemy, who has done nothing to us, comes after them with a gun, we put ourselves and our families in their mess. Do you know, when we lock up criminals, we become apart of their hit list. If they cannot get us, they will get vulnerable ones, the wives and children. We automatically put ourselves in harms way. We're not always with back- up. We do not have a bullet proof vest on at all times, and some officers' department will not allow them to have their weapon at all times.

People are on the outside looking in, so they cannot stereotype us or our work. Critics do not know the pressure that an officer goes through. All over the world, everyday, we arrest people who make threats to kill us, our parents, wives, and children, but which of the threats will be carried out? When will the attempt occur? Where will I be when they try it? Will they try me or my family? Will we be shopping at a family outing, at church, where, when and how will the threat occur? Did we really lock up someone who believes in revenge? These are the questions that rest in our minds. Can you handle the pressure of being an officer? People are so quick to criticize officers, and say if they were a cop what they would do. We are faced with pressure situations that they could not handle. They will simply buckle.

Could you imagine getting a phone call from someone that you have arrested and they tell you, that if you had moved two more steps to the left, he would have slit you throat. Well in 1998, it happened to a friend of mind, he describes his clothing and the very small logo on the sleeve. The perpetrator told him that he need to stop sleeping until 3 a.m. and opening the patio door letting the dog out. Can you handle the very fact that your worst enemy knows your everyday activities? This is just some of the pressure that we endure, so we do not have time to hear critic's petit complaints?

Christmas Eve 2001, on a dark, curvy, and lonely Jeffries Rd, a hunter reported a burned vehicle in the field. Well, Sgt. Leroy Whitehead, the officer who responded, thought that it was just a stolen vehicle that had burned.

Little that he knew, upon arrival, he noticed a totally charred skeleton. It was totally burned beyond recognition. It turned out to be a young black male. Whitehead said he thought, now some child is waiting for their dad to come home. It's another case of another young male without a father. The family got the news that the person is possibly a relative. They began to call the Sheriffs' Department to find out if it was true that their relative may be dead. We couldn't confirm that because at that time, investigators could not determine if it was black or white, or male or female. For days the family desired closure, but until the department could get some sure information, they could not answer all of the family's questions.

We felt their pain and wished that we could do something about it. There was nothing we could do but wait. Have you ever wanted to help someone so bad but there was nothing you could do? All of their burdens fell on us because they wanted to find out who could have been so cruel to kill him and especially in that way. Whoever was responsible, it will be an officer who comfronts and apprehend the perpetrator. I wonder if any critics want to face someone who is that cruel and evil. If so, there are positions open. Do they want to take the chance of this perpetrator finding them before they find him? Well, that's the chance that we have to take. Do you know criminals know who the cops are when we don't know who they are?

I'm in a small town, so the things that we see are a bit smaller than what cops in larger cities see. The types of people they deal with are more dangerous than what we deal with. The Texas Seven, they were men who were already convicted felons. In 2001, they escaped and went on a rampage of crimes including murdering a cop. They had the whole United States in fear. They made other attempts to kill cops, but they fell short and they kept fleeing. While citizens locked their doors and looked out of the windows in fear, Cops looked in cars, establishments etc. to find them. It's the officers who said, "I will put my life on the line for the people of the U.S. The photos that we were issued were taken a few years prior to the escape. We were looking for seven different people. After they were apprehended, new pictures were shown, and they looked nothing like the photos given to us. They could have walked up to us and shot us. Danger hangs all around us. Would you like to be in that type of danger zone?

Would critics have liked to come face to face with the alleged flesh eater, Jeffry Dumbner, no, because they would have been afraid thinking that they would have become victims. Well, if he had caught them, they probably would have been eaten. These are people that cops have to come in contact with first, just so everyone else can feel safe. We are proud of what we do, and any one who violates the law will be dealt with.

In the summer of the 1990's, two fishermen in a boat were fishing but to there surprise, a plastic bag was caught up in the hook. When they pulled it in, they saw something that they never thought they would see. It was an upper torso. The person's torso was placed into a plastic bag. It was reported to officers. Investigators called in a dive team and they located other body parts in separate bags. It was that of a man. The parts were found and officers had to help put the body together in a bag. Can your stomach handle a cut up dismembered body that had been under water in a plastic bag for months, well, officers had to.

In the mid-1990's in Southern Mississippi,

neighbors reported a loud shot sound. Upon arrival, officers were advised that the man came home but did not leave. They said shortly afterwards they heard the shot; officers used forced entry and saw what looked like spaghetti on the wall. They went over to the rocking chair and saw a rifle on the floor and what appeared to be a male sitting in the chair. When they got in front of the chair they saw a male body from neck down. The head was blown into bits and pieces. There was only a fraction of a jaw left attached to the neck, because he had committed suicide. Life's disappointments had gotten the best of him. Would you like to see some of that fragment on the wall in one of America's favorite dishes (spaghetti), well, that's what officers see when intestines and brains are forced outward by gunshots. We can't eat spaghetti for a long time. If critics would see the awful scenes, I believe they would complain less, but if they feel that they can do better, then they should apply because more officers are needed.

Witnesses

If a person have witnessed a crime or know information about one, they are very important to us. They are the key that locks up criminals for good. They are the answers to our and the victims prayers. Some family is waiting on them to come forward so they can have closure. They can be a big help to us, but for some reason they will not help us. There are families that expect us to solve cases, but we are not God. We do not know everything. We need witnesses to help solve the cases. We're not there when a crime happens, so the people that know information about a crime, WE NEED YOU!!!

How would you feel, if the person you love the most, whether it is your child, spouse, best friend or parents were murdered and you heard that someone had information about it, but they wouldn't come forward? Ask yourself, how would I feel? Sometimes it's your own family that has the information. What if they didn't want to talk? One eyewitness can make the difference in the closing of a case. He/she can seal the conviction of a criminal.

Some people feel, if they come forward, then they'll be in jeopardy. Well, let me enlighten them on something. They are in less danger by talking. If a perpetrator saw someone looking at him or think someone saw him because they were so close by, they are going to find the witness and kill them, so the life they save just may be their own.

When a perpetrator find an eyewitness, then no one will know what happened to the first victim or them, because what they know will go to the ground with them. Someone else was a victim instead of you? Do you know why, It's because someone else crossed paths with him before you did. The perpetrator probably was headed to the house down the street until they spotted a quicker catch, but guess what, just because someone else won't come forward and tell us what they say, they may be next on the killers list, and he or she just might succeed.

Think about it. If someone has robbed, raped and killed another person and is facing a capital murder charge, and they know that there was one witness, he/she is probably not going to live. I'm sorry for that witness if he/she thinks that they may get away forever.

Why are some people in a neighborhood watch area, if they are not going to tell what they see that is wrong in the neighborhood? They just want to make sure that their property is being watched. "Red Alert" Be careful who you have watching you and your property. They may not be watchers, they may be stalkers. I've always been told that if you sow it, you will reap it.

Whatever a person does to someone else, that person or someone else will do it to them. Whenever a person refuses to help someone when they're in need, odds are, they want receive help when they're in need. So, if eyewitnesses keep on being quiet when someone else needs them. I promise you, when someone in their family becomes victims, they will never find out what happened.

These are the same people that have the nerve to criticize cops for not solving a crime when they have the answers and want come forward. At least we are trying. They are too afraid to come forward. If they are not careful, they will go from witness to being a participant in the crime, and when they do, we're coming for them. Then, "what you gone do, when we come for you"? You best believe, when a person commit acts of crime or assist in it, some way or another, evidence is left at the scene, and/or they have taken some away from the scene. So, if we receive a tip on them, the participants and their property, will be tested by people who can take a very small spot of fiber and link them to a crime. They are our (cops) best help. They are called Forensic Scientist.

Forensics

Crime just doesn't pay these days, thanks to modern day technology and some expert scientists. These are the people that we (cops) rely on when there's only small pieces of fiber or DNA to work with. These are people that link the smallest clues to the largest crimes. They see things that the eye can't. They are our key witness. In January 1988 a body was found in Butler Ohio River. Orange carpet fibers were found on the body. The body was eventually recovered and cops had no witness and very little clues. Forensics scientists begin to process the fibers on the body. They concluded that the fiber was from a carpet that was traced back the J&B Stephens Manufacturing Company. It also was narrowed down to the only places that sold that type of carpet, then narrowed to a particular area, and then to the only buyer of the carpet in the area. The finger was then pointed at a suspect Rob Bueller who had killed Krita Harson, loaded her in his van with orange carpet, and threw her into a lake. He was arrested, convicted and sentenced to life in prison. As you can see, no matter how much perpetrators try to carefully plan a crime, they'll leave or take some evidence with them. The same fibers found on the carpet were found inside the husband's van. Can you image being killed by your spouse for insurance money? Well, neither do several spouses but it happen.

Forensic Pathologists are witnesses who see the crime after it is solved. They may not be able to specify what happened on the scene, but they can say what tool was used to commit the crime, how far the perpetrator was from the victim while the crime was being committed, how long the person has been dead.

When the human body encounters more than one fatal act, they can tell which one actually caused the murder. These are the witnesses that make criminals say, "I'm guilty of the crime that I'm being charged with". They will stand bold and say exactly what happened, where as a regular eyewitness will be afraid to talk. We appreciate their fine works and accurate judgment. They help investigators to solve crimes and nail criminals. Our hats are off to them being key witnesses, we really appreciate them.

Forensic Scientists are a really big help to us. We need professional and highly educated officials like them to speak on our behalf at times. Their testimonies in court help judges with their decision making. Officers are only sent to training for a few months and get trained through the department, whereas their years give them an advantage. Their findings and testimonies help us to speak against the fancy terminology and reverse psychology of the people who gets pleasure in burning an officer on the stands. They are lawyer

Part IV
What Bracket Do They Fall In
(Winner or Loser)

Lawyers

Any law abiding citizen that makes an honest living is all right with me, but were I have a problem is that the law breakers can <u>commit</u> any crime, and for some reason they can get a lawyer for free to represent them, It's part of their constitutional rights. If they can't afford one, the taxpayers will do it for them. The victims that the criminals violate are the same ones who pay for his or her attorney, I don't know who figured that out. If your neighbor is a victim of a robbery, and the perpetrator, is caught, then the perpetrator gets the privilege of being represented with that same neighbors tax dollars.

Being a lawyer is a profession, but it is also a criminal's escape route. Who don't know that lawyers are more educated than police officers? Everything that we are taught in a basic class academy, lawyers are taught that same literature, so they find a strategy to beat that. They use loop wholes and fancy words to fool the jury. Most juries are not highly educated; they are picked from the community and sent to court. From what I have seen, a lot of them have not finished high school. A six-letter word sounds impressing to them. They think that they are making a decision on guilt or innocence, but they are actually taking sides with the best sounding and convincing lawyer.

We have crimes, and evidence to support our

61

cases, but the fact that we are human, we make mistakes. They use our little mistakes and capitalize on them. Just because we have been one minute off of dispatcher's log time and misspelled a word, they will convince the jury and judge that our testimonies are not accurate, and inconsistent, so what, that a word was misspelled. We find ourselves thinking, we're not in a spelling B, it's a criminal case. If we have a dead, dismembered body that was last seen by an eyewitness with the suspect with him, just minutes before a victim dies, and part of him or his property was left at the crime scene. There should not be a concern about a misspelled word. Lawyers have to know the truth. I am sure it is required that their client be honest with you. They walk around feeling proud of themselves, but they are allowing a killer to walk again? They may get a perpetrator off, but he knows that his attorney knows the truth, and he just might make his attorney be his next victim.

We watch them in the courtroom with their nice suit and their scuffed looking shoes. They come in court with their demands and requests, and they only hurt the society. If a drunk driver has killed someone, the best representation for him is to have him plead guilty and pay for his mistakes. He need to go back to school for drunks and get clean, but lawyers request for a copy of the Intoxilizer 5000's calibration log as well as a copy of our DUI and field sobriety certificate in the court room. Intoxilizer 5000 is a state certified machine that determines the blood alcohol contents of an alleged drunk driver.

Sometimes we have lost cases because we did not have the certificate in our hands. But I don't consider it a lost because that night, I took a drunk off the street, and they paid a tow bill, but lawyers put him back on the streets for good. Does winning the case always make them a winner? Are they concerned about their win or a brokenhearted mother's lost? So far, what bracket do they fall in, W or L.

When they put a drunk back on the streets, he feels that he has defeated us and with his lawyer, he can do it again. They are going to go back out and kill someone else. What purpose does it serves for us to arrest them and they set them free. Would they take their murder case if they had just killed their child? It would not be about the money then. They try to present us to the judge and jury to be less than intelligent. They take our statements and reports, find a small mistake and use it against us. We are not the ones who are on trial. Their arrogance shows, but they do not impress me. I wonder how they feel when their client makes the news again for the same crime that they were defending him on. They may win the battle in court but they will loose the everyday fight. Yeah, they helped them through court, but they hurt everyone else in society. They are under worked, over staffed and over paid, while we are over worked, under staffed, and under paid.
We put in extra, unpaid hours to make sure all of our statements are correct, our evidence is tagged and in proper order just to put away a criminal, but sometimes because of who their attorney is, criminals go free. Not all the time is it the lawyers, but politics plays a major role in conviction. Regardless if the person is a law officer, or a regular citizen, no one is above the law.

POLITICIANS

This is a really big problem in small counties.
The calls that we respond to are not always the same
criminals that no one knows or care about. Some of our
worst citizens are related to someone in a high position.
Whenever they do wrong, they come to their rescue.
Their behavior will never change if power pushers keep
getting them out of trouble. The only thing they are
asking for is for them to be found dead. If they keep
committing different types of acts, but nothing is
happening to them, someone will grow tired of them
and take action themselves. This is especially to the
people working in the department. Some of them have
the worst relatives in the county. They are always
committing crimes and their so-called law enforcement
relatives have attitudes with an officer for doing his job.
As long as it's someone that they don't know or
someone they do not like, then we are doing such a
good job to arrest them. They are fence straddles and do
not know if they are with us or against us, but they
don't have to decide because I don't have anything to
do with them nor do I trust them. They're not on the
right side, but they are criminals. When an individual
assist someone in their trouble, then they are just as
guilty as the criminal. It doesn't matter how long they
have been there or what position they hold, they're
wrong.

Good officer are not favored most of the time
because he (she) comes to work to do a job and not join
a click. The power, money and sex stays in the click,
the ones who are not really team players. I heard a man
says that P.M.S. (power, money, and sex) is a man's
thing. I agree with him more than 100%. It's not a
woman thing. It's a man's thing. As long as a man can
call the shots, make the most money, and sleep with

more than one woman, he is satisfied. There's no love amongst them because love is not spelled with a PMS, but a good officer can easily spell love because of what he stands for. He's Loyal, Obedient, Vital, and he's Ethical. That's the type of officer that all departments NEED. This type of officer is rejected all around this country because most of the people's mentality has been so corrupt that they think that wrong is O.K. and right is not. Fault should not be found on them for being men that stands on their own. Just because a person is a male over the age of 21, produced a baby, and hold a job, that doesn't make him a man. A man will stand and hold his house together well. That is a man. A person does not have to be 21 to be a man. The political war has caused the good to go bad and the bad to go worse.

Sometimes it is the so- called "big timers" that get caught up in illegal activities. The law does not exclude them. Just because their bank account is large because of all the people they've ripped off, that's not a reason to let them free when they commit a crime. They need to pay their debt to society. I have seen some evade police because they are one of the following, governor, senator, judge etc., and they think that they do not have to stop until they get where they are going. That is wrong. The Sheriff's is the highest, elected, law enforcement officer in our town and in 1999 he was arrested and paid his debts to society. Why can't they? Most politicians' relatives are often in trouble, because somewhere they got the message that their high positioned relatives are so powerful that they can fix anything. Until politicians do better, their relatives are not going to do better. They make many promises. One of them is to slow crime but they indulge in crime by rescuing the relatives all the time. They know if they will rewind those lying promises that they give doing election time, they will find that they made up a bunch of lies. They only mean themselves good. All year long, we don't see or hear from most of them unless they are complaining about our work performance. They show up at our church once the whole time that they are running for office. Our leader can't get them to do any work for him. They will not send donations, and most of them will not visit. But when election time comes, they are breaking the church doors down with their little speeches and trying to buy us offerings. Maybe blacks, whites, and other races of politicians think we are ignorant of why they come. We know why they are there, but it would be wrong not to let them in, but might I worn them, God doesn't accept their offering, the church may, but God doesn't.

They may win an election, but are they really being a winner. Have they totally led their children down the right path? Do they put their relatives in place when they're wrong? Do they promote by employees appearance and performance or by whoever is in their click. When they constantly rescue their children out of trouble after they constantly violate other people and their property, are they in the win or lose bracket? When they promote someone for sexual and other favors, or give them big raises in return for something else. Are they being a winner or loser? If they think that their answer is "W" than they are self-righteous and full of themselves. How can a leader reprimand their employees for doing the same thing that they're involved in? I have really lost a lot of respect for a lot of politicians because they only help those that are friends and relatives.

When perpetrators violate a politician or his family and they're not caught, we are criticized, well, how do they (politicians) think someone else feels when their criminal child does something illegal and they are allowed to rescue them because of their position? There is no difference in their troubled child and someone else. If they keep coming to their rescue, and keep living, they will see that they are only losing.

Wives of Cops

In whatever I do, I desire my wife's support, from lifting a feather to moving a mountain. A wife should be a total helpmate to her husband, especially the wife of a cop. It takes a special type of woman to be the wife of a cop.

When I first told my wife that I was interested in being an officer, the look on her face was, please anything but that, but she never disagreed verbally. She told me if that is what I wanted, she is right there with me. When my mother, in-laws and other family members questioned my decision, my wife supported me. When I found out that I would be going to the police Academy, I immediately came home and told her. I told her that I will be leaving for a week at a time and will be home each weekend. She said we will miss you, but we support you. When I left, I left her to all of the chores, the kids, and to take care of home, and it took a special woman to do that. Every time I came home, things were in place. It took a big sacrifice to take on the whole load, but she did it. Sometimes frustration sat in with her but she would not give up. Each weekend that I came home, she would count down the weeks and say it is not long now. The day I graduated, she packed up our three kids and drove two and a half hours to support me. She was looking so beautiful, as well as my kids. They made me proud. I could not have done it without her. This was just a small sacrifice compared to the one that is made everyday. Wives, in everything that officers do, please support them.

When we go out at night, we need a clear mind and a clear conscious. It's imperative that wives support him because sometimes they are his only support. There are things that he's going to face that only she can help him through. It's essential that wives don't give them a hard time. Even if they do have a disagreement, they need to make sure before he goes out to work, that they have gotten it straight. She should never let him leave with a mind set, that she is angry with him. That can cause him to make a bad decision because his mind is not on his job, but it's on the problem that he left home with. The decision can cause him and the whole family hurt and pain. It can cause him to be sued personally, and that can effect the whole family. So, she should never let him leave without telling him that she is sorry and that she loves him, and mean it when she says it. That should never be allowed to happen, because there is no guarantee that he will make it back home. Once he goes out the door, it's praying time. She should pray that God will keep him and bring him home safe and unharmed. It would be a sad thought that her husband dies and she didn't say goodbye or she love him because she felt like raising hell before he left.

They should never make him feel that he is not wanted. When he feels that she don't love him and he knows that most of the citizens don't like him, what is it for him to do. The officer gets caught up in what he loves and what he has lost. This sometimes causes an officer to commit suicide. Cops rank high among the suicides. He loves his wife and his job but it seems neither loves him. If she doesn't want him, let him know, and I am sure he could find someone who would love and appreciate him.

There are women out there that will be glad to make him feel loved. If it's nothing major that she's experiencing, she should never keep her body from him. Whether she wants to or not, if he asked to be intimate, she should give it to him. If she continues the lack of sex, it doesn't justify it, but it can cause him to commit adultery. She should take care of him, because there are women who are waiting for a good husband. Some just want an officer to be intimate with them. Some officers are not concerned about other women they just want their wives to do their wifely duties. Situations can quickly and easily arise and if the wife is not being intimate with her husband, then the wrong decision can be made. In the winter of 2001, I responded to a female that was violating her restraining order. When I caught up with the lady, she was told that she was going to jail, so she began to offer some type of sexual favors to let her go, but it didn't work. Wives don't get caught up. There are female officers also that are feeling unloved. One slow and lonely night can cause their thoughts to go beyond partnership.

I am pleased with my wife and her support. She takes a heavy load off of me. She listens to me as well as gives me advice. She makes sure my uniform is pressed and all of my brass is shining. She often tells me how good I look to her in my uniform. That itself is an encouragement. One day I asked her, what do you feel when I leave for work? She responded with this. "I watch you from start to finish as you spit shine your shoes, shine your brass, and put on your uniform. When you finish putting everything on, I think, no one looks better in a Sheriff's uniform than you. As you go to the truck and I come out behind you to hug you. I began to pray, "Lord please bring him home safe and unharmed, as I tell you to be careful and I love you." For every siren I hear, I pray harder that you are kept safe. Every phone call, I am hoping that the call I am receiving is not the one every officers' wife dreads, saying that you have been shot. When there is a knock at the door, I am hoping that it's not your boss saying, "Mrs. Davis, I have something to tell you, Officer Davis has been badly wounded. I can't help but think how much you sacrifice when you walk out of that door for work. You take the chance of never seeing your wife or children again just to protect and serve in your community where people care absolutely nothing about you".

There is no guarantee that we will come home, so I urge the cop's wives to be in place where they can be contacted if this time comes. It would really be a pathetic thought if his wife was notified of such incident at a motel with another man or in the nightclub. I wonder if some of those unfaithful wives of cops are going to change their ways. Will they be a helpmate to them, support them until death, and be a winner, or will they keep being difficult and mistreating them and end up loosing them? The bracket that they fall in is totally up to those individuals.

Fence Straddlers

They are the reason that people have this perception of us. It's they that gives and has given us a bad name.

Years ago, police officers didn't have to be highly educated. All they had to be was big and tall. The solution for getting people to cooperate back then was to beat it out of them. Law enforcement has totally changed, it's a profession and we are expected to be professionals. Physical abuse is not an option in law enforcement. What sense does it make to beat a man with a stick? There are tactics and techniques to use when placing someone under arrest. OC spray is affective. If it's not, then they should call for back up to get it under control. If they're out numbered, then that's different, they are to use any means necessary to survive. If his life is in danger, then he should do what ever to live, but to beat a man because he has the power is not acceptable. If an officer gets pleasure out of physical abuse, then he needs a reality check. That's police brutality, and he should be charged. If they're officers, than they should conduct themselves like one. If not they should go ahead and be a criminal. Officers can't straddle the fence with this profession. How can an officer arrest someone for assault if they're going to do it?

Just because someone else makes them mad, that's not a justifiable reason for beating someone. They should leave their problems at home, or maybe they just like to beat people. If so, they better change their ways. They'll find themselves paying for the rest of their lives. A winner will drop what's wrong for what's right, but a loser will continue to do what's wrong.If they don't change, I know what bracket they'll fall in.

Some corrupt officers are thieves. Why take from someone, just because they're too drunk to know what's going on, that's their property. They need to be careful when they take something from someone, because they don't know who have a camera on them or in their car, but regardless if they have one or not, they should have enough police ethics in them not to bother their property.

When a person is cuffed, why would an officer beat, kick, or even slam his head on the patrol car? That doesn't make any sense. When officers cuff someone, they have just taken their right to freedom, there's no need to hit them. Why don't they try to hit him when his hands are free, because they know that they'll get whipped? Officers must have some confidence in themselves that they can control a situation without being abusive. If they are doing anything other than placing them in their unit when they cuff them, then they are violating their Civil Rights. As long as this type of activity continues, as officers, we will never get anywhere. We will never gain the respect of citizens again. We are trying to correct the problem, not add to it. I've seen several good officers get caught on camera like that. Why would they throw away their careers for the pleasure of misusing someone? I encourage them do not be a loser, it's not worth it.

Just because an officer knows someone or maybe owes someone for some reason, there is no need to say something happened and it didn't. In other words they shouldn't falsify a report just to satisfy their friend or their family. If a friend was in the wrong, then it need to be written as their friend was in fault, and if their friend doesn't understand. Then he or she was never their friend. Falsifying a report will result in termination and prosecution. Even if they want to get even with someone who has done them wrong, officers can't add to their complainant testimony. They need to write it up just like the complainant said it: This will keep an officer from incriminating himself. There's no need to lose a fight, that's already won. If an officer lie about a case, and it comes to trial 4 years later, will they remember those same lies when those defense attorneys begin to drill them? When they begin to lie, they will get burned on the stands. These actions also lead to other doorways of evil.

When Christians begin to get off track, they refer back to their Bibles. The word of God will correct an individual if a person is sincere in being a Christian. If an officer finds himself getting off track, then he should refer back to his state statues. If he is really trying to stay in line, then he needs to read it. It's a law officers Bible. If they just can't seem to get it right, they need to go to counseling, admit their problem(s) and the counselor will help them deal with it. If that does not help, I recommend them to try another profession. Quitting doesn't always make a person a loser. I've always been told, if you quit some thing, you are a loser. But in this particular situation, if you quit, then you are a winner. Law enforcement is not for everyone, and everyone in the uniform is not necessarily a good law enforcement officer. I encourage them to make the right choice today whether they will be a winner or loser.

Some people think that all officers became cops to throw their weight and power around, and that's not the case. Some of us have done hard labor all of our lives and we didn't get good pay or benefits. Whenever someone is being interviewed for a job, the first two questions that he/she asks are, How much it pays, and what type of benefits are there? That's my reason for accepting the job of an officer. I was very interested in the benefits. All officers are not corrupt, but unfortunately we are categorized with corrupt officers. Now, there is no justification for corruption, but you must sympathize with a man that's trying to take care of his family and the county keeps giving slap in the face raises. These men know there's money in the county and they want a part of it. In Tunica, there has been a history of Sheriff/Deputy corruption, and a lot of people often ask why, well the reason for the corruption is this, **NO MONEY mixed with greed,** it is the breeding ground to police corruption. A lot of cops are from the streets, but they made a change expecting to live a comfortable and straight life, but because there are no good salaries or raises, then they go back to what took care of them for years, the streets. It's called a hustle. So, the ones who are in charge of giving the raises (**THE SHERIFF &THE BOARD OF SUPERVISORS**) either do not care about corruption, or are part-takers of it and that's been proven over the years. Tunica should not be plagued by the same corruption term after term, whoever is in a position to change it, need to get busy or get ready to experience the same thing. If I knew that I could solve corruption in my town, I would stop it immediately by giving my officers a good salary. This is what's puzzling to me, most of the times, before becoming a Sheriff, a person will serve as an officer, so they know how it feels to live off $16-$20,000 in their house **A YEAR**, but they will get in office, and give the same raises that they often complained about as a regular officer, I don't get it. I will admit, some officers have really made it bad for good officers, but don't use that as an excuse not to give officers raises, because some of us do things decently and orderly. We do business the right way, but sometimes we still hear negative talk no matter how right we try to do it, so the critics that feel that they can do better, then I'll give them the chance. Just remember; when you answer these questions, there's no pressure on you. If you get the wrong answer, or make the wrong decision, nothing happens to you, but if we (officers) make a bad decision, it can and will come back to haunt us. The pressure that's on us when we make our decisions is crucial.

  The next ten pages are different scenarios. Answer them as if you were a cop that had to make those decisions and see will you past the test. You must get them all correct or you fail. It only takes one mistake that will cost us millions, our careers, prison time, or our lives.

Cop Test

You have been wanting to catch Roger Coleslaw for a long time. Roger Coleslaw is the biggest drug dealer in your town. He has come next door to you selling to the junkies that stays up all night. You finally get a tip that the biggest deal ever will be going down tonight. Coleslaw is going to sell 15 bags of uncut cocaine totaling one million dollars in street value. You heard that a red mustang would meet him in the town park at three a.m. You got your other officers with you and you are ready. At three in the morning, there is no red car or even close to the park, but you see Coleslaw leaving the service station at
3 a.m. A junkie that you have never dealt with before told you that they were sure it was going down. Coleslaw is cruising toward the park where his house is, during 20 mph through a 20 mph zone, and keeping a straight line with everything in place. What should you do?

        A. Stop him before he reaches the park.
        B. Stop him after he gets to the park.
        C. Just let him go with all of the dope in the
car.
        D. Stop the car, get the dope, and turn it in.

You are patrolling when you notice a violation occur. So you turn around and get behind the car and pull it over. When you pulled the car over, a wild looking, and crazy acting man gets out of the car with a handgun in his hand, and Just so happens, the local news team is driving by and decided they will film the traffic stop just to show the world how professional the officers are in their town. Now, you have asked him five times already to drop the gun. You can clearly see. It is daytime and the gun is visible. "This is the last warning." This is what you have made up in your mind. Drop the gun and he still does not drop it. What do you do next?

A: Shoot him in the leg, why?
B. Shoot him in the chest, why?
C. Shoot him where the gun hand is, why?
D. Shoot him right in the head, why?

You are doing a routine check at the local factory, when you see your neighbors Johnny and Tina Turnip seed. You wave and keep going, because you know they are at work. When you make it to the local neighborhood, you see Johnny Turnip seed Jr. He starts to run, when he sees you, when you catch him, he has 5 -dime bags of marijuana on him. You bring him to juvenile where you get all of his personal information. You know he is selling for someone who is an adult, and you want to know who so bad. How many more questions should you ask him that pertains to the drugs?

A. As many as you need to ask.
B. 5
C. 3
D. 2
E. As many as you want

Melvin Butterbean is a big drug dealer who is very careful when he drives. Every time you see him, he is doing the posted speed limit with his seat belt on. You know he keep drugs in the car because a good source of yours, heard him tell someone that. So one day you see him, and he is driving fast and peeling tires. When you pull him over, and begin to interview him, you ask him are there any drugs in the car, he says, "no." Then you ask him, can you search the vehicle to see if there are any drugs in the car. He says, "No." What should you do? He is a valid driver.

     A. Write a ticket for reckless driving and let him go.

     B. Search the car anyway to find the dope.

     C. Search the car and write him a ticket.

     D. None of the above

You get a call of a shoplifter. The dispatcher tells you that the manager called and said, "Someone in a red mustang GT grabbed two big packages of pork steakes and ran out the store. When they give his location, you are already in that area. You see him and get behind him and the chase is on. Your partner joins in and both of you try to block him in. He spins that GT around and made both of you look bad in front of your family and friends. Your whole family is laughing at how he made you two look bad. He gets back on the highway and gets up to 105 mph. How far do you chase him at that speed?

     A. Until he pulls over to safety.

     B. 5 miles.

C. As far as the next county.

D. Let him wreck the car and get him later.

E. None of the above

To These Questions

Remember, you have the answers right here. We don't have the answers right before us. You can take your time and think about the right answer. We have only a split second to make a decision. Just think, you can get the wrong answer, but as officers, we cannot.

Your Sheriff's name is Terry Egg roll. His son's name is Larry Egg roll. You received a call from a dispatcher saying Larry Egg roll just killed someone and ran to an unknown location. You are in route to the call, and your sheriff and all of his appointees are on the way. You are the first officer on scene. You immediately secure the area. You have the evidence of murder, and possible murder weapons and there is evidence of what the suspect left. Who should you let inside the scene without getting their name before the crime scene investigator?

    A. Only the Sheriff, why?

    B. The Sheriff and his chief deputy, why?

    C. All of his appointees, why?

    D. Your immediate supervisor, why?

    E. None of these above, why?

Remember, when you answer these scenarios, you have the answers in front of you, but we do not. We have to come up with answers, and fast. You can take as much time as you need, miss all of the questions and no head is on the chopping block.

A suicidal man is walking around outside saying he was going to kill himself. He walks with the gun to his head and then stop, sits down and put the gun in his mouth. You are trying to convince him that shooting himself is not good. You and your partners have your guns drawn. No one is outside but you, your partners and the suicidal man. He yells out in five seconds, he is going to pull the trigger. He begins to count down. Before he gets to one, what should you do, before he shoots himself?

> **A.** Shoot him in the gun hand, why?
> **B.** Shoot him in the foot, why?
> **C.** Shoot him in the leg, why?
> **D.** None of these above, why?

You are on your way to do a routine check at the biggest game of the year, (homecoming). You then get a 911- Hang up Call and the dispatcher advised that they heard some commotion in the background. Then you advised the dispatcher that you are on your way to the call. Halfway there, the dispatcher says, be advised someone called from the residence and said everything is O.K. You are ready to get back to that game. The dispatcher said everything is all right. What should you do?

> **A.** Nothing, go back to the game, the dispatcher said everything is O.K.

B. Drive by the residence

C. Go in the residence.

D. Get the phone number from the dispatcher and call personally to see if everything is O.K

E. None of the above.

What is the first thing you do if you drive up and notice a lifeless body, after you report it to the dispatcher?

A. Call the Sheriff

B. Rope off the area and secure it

C. Call the investigator that deals with homicides

D. Call the coroner

E. None of the above.

Put this traffic stop in chronological order

1. Greet them
2. Allow them to tell you why they committed the violation.
3. Ask for drivers' license, registration and insurance.
4. Tell them why they were being stopped.
5. Pull the car over with blue lights and sirens.
6. Check their information
7. Give them a warning-written or verbal.

Once you run a drivers license and they comes back suspended, what should you   do?

A. Let them go, and tell them they need to get them reinstated.

B. Write them a ticket and then let them go.

C. Take them to jail and book them in\

D. None of the above

Summary

Law enforcement officers are criticized everyday. We do the best that we were trained in, especially in the time that we had to accomplish it. We get a lot of criticism from negative people. They complain but they could not handle this job.

With all the things that we see, go through and experience, we have to deal with them. So, if you are a critic that complain and criticize, ask yourself, "Can I fill their shoes." I mean really, "Can you fill our shoes?" This question is to the public and for everyone who criticizes our work, and thinks they can do better.

We go though a lot and it sometimes take a lot out of us. Some of these things most people cannot handle, but they will complain at the way we handle it. We do our best, but it just doesn't satisfy some people. So, if you think **you can fill our shoes**, then go to your local department and see if you can handle being an officer. See if you can:

Past the background check, past the police academy, deal with what we see everyday and the frustrations of the job,(Politics, Lawyers, Judges, Lack of money, Crooked Cops, and Complaining Citizens) and then see if by the end of your career, will you retire or resign without losing a suit, going to jail, or dying in the line of duty.

Answers to the questions and scenarios

1. C-you must have probable cause to stop a vehicle, even though you got a tip, it was from a "junkie" that you have never had any dealings with. His or her credibility is no good in a courtroom. You may get the dope, but not the conviction because Coleslaw was not doing anything wrong when you stopped him. The junkie is probably mad because Coleslaw would not let him/her get dope on credit.

2. Neither-If you chose A,B,C or D, then the whole world watched you shoot a man who was possibly deaf and couldn't talk, and was not opposing any type of immediate threat to you or anyone else. **Possible Scenario:** He never pointed the gun. He had written a note in his car saying, "I cannot hear or talk, but I found this gun and wanted to give it to my good friends, the police.

3. F- You cannot question a juvenile without a parent present.

4. A- You cannot search a vehicle without the driver's consent to search, unless there is a smell of burned marijuana, or the K-9(dog) indicate the presence of drugs.

5. E-The crime was not serious enough to pursue at 100 mph.

6. E-No one comes inside your crime scene without getting their names until the crime scene investigator takes over the scene and gives authorization, not even to the Sheriff. If the suspect is his son, and you let him in, he just may tamper with the evidence to see his son go free.

7. D-It may sound cruel, but if his mind is made up

to kill himself, there is nothing you can say or do to stop him, let him kill himself. If you shoot and wound him, he may become desperate and kill himself or shoot someone else, and you will be fire, sued, and charged with aggravated assault..

8. C-If there is commotion over the phone on a 911-hand up, you must gain entry to assure safety. Anyone could have made that call, or be forced to make that call. It could have been the perpetrator buying time to finish his intentions.

9. B-If you call everyone to the scene before you get it roped off, chances are, evidence will be destroyed.

10. 5,1,4,2,3,6,7

11. C-If you let them go, and then they go up the street and cause a fatality, you are civilly liable because you were advised that the state had temporarily taken that person's driving privilege, but you still allowed them to drive.

This book serves as a test to people who think that this job is easy and that the duties contain therein are simple. Most of the time, regardless of how we handle a situation, it's not acceptable to many people. Everyday people are tested in some way or the other, and it is up to that individual to overcome that test. I must applaud all officers including myself for a job well done, because we endure many tests, the ones at home, and every job related one.

This book also describes incidents that occur in the field, many that offer a life time of hurt, pain and soul searching. So before you criticize another cop, remember that you heard it straight from the horse's mouth, that life as a cop can be very challenging. And the next time you hear someone criticize an officer, think deeply about everything you've read and ask them, CAN YOU FILL THEIR SHOES?

I would like to thanks the officers that I interviewed for sharing their experiences.

I would like to extend my thanks to the director and his staff from the Mississippi Law Enforcement Officers Training Academy for preparing us physically and mentally.

I'd like to thank Mary Jackson who allowed me to use photos of her wounded daughter.

Special thanks to the librarians of the Robert C. Erwin Library

Very Special Thanks

I thank God almighty for the ability to physically and mentally complete this task. I also thank him for his promises that he has allowed me to receive. I'd like to send a

Very Special thanks to my wife Teresa and my children, Kenneth Davis, Jr. Destiny Knakia Davis, and Carlos R. Johnson for their sacrifice of time so I could finish this project.

I would like to thank my spiritual leaders for their prayers

Very Special thanks to my mother for the many years of endurance, sacrifices, influence and the constant will to live saved. You are one of my greatest encouragements.

All names and business names have been altered. Any similarities in names or incidents, are totally coincidental.

Direct book orders can be accomplished by calling,

(Kenneth Davis, Sr.) @ (228)-313-2647. Enjoy your

reading and Thank You for your purchase.

Tools for the Shoes

Tools for the Shoes

Printed in the United States
by Baker & Taylor Publisher Services